A Dorling Kindersley Book

Conceived, edited and designed by DK Direct Limited

Note to parents

What's Inside? My Body is designed to help young children
understand the fascinating inner workings of the human body.
It shows the most important features like the heart,
the lungs and the skeleton, and explains in simple terms
what each part does. It is a book for you and your child
to read and talk about together, and to enjoy.

Designers Juliette Norsworthy and Sonia Whillock
Typographic Designer Nigel Coath
Editors Simon Bell and Alexandra Parsons
Design Director Ed Day
Editorial Director Jonathan Reed

Illustrator Richard Manning
Photographers Steve Gorton and Paul Bricknell
Writer Angela Royston

First published in Great Britain in 1991
by Dorling Kindersley Limited,
9 Henrietta Street, London WC2E 8PS

Reprinted 1995

A CIP catalogue record for this book is available from the British Library.

ISBN 0-86318-694-7

Printed in Italy

WHAT'S INSIDE?

MY BODY

DORLING KINDERSLEY
LONDON • NEW YORK • STUTTGART

UNDER MY SKIN

I know how my body looks on the outside, but I wonder
what is inside? My skin and flesh are soft and under them
I can feel hard, knobbly bones.

My hair grows
longest and thickest
on my head.

Skin covers my body like
a stretchy suit. It stops
germs getting inside.

I can feel bones
all over my body,
except here on
my tummy.

Hundreds of small,
fine hairs grow
all over my skin.
They help to keep
me warm.

My bones are like a big coat-hanger. They give me my shape and keep my insides in place.

Here is my headbone. It is called the skull. It holds and protects my brain like a shell holding a nut.

These are my rib bones. They make a cage to protect my heart and lungs.

This is my backbone. It is made of lots of smaller bones joined together, so that I can bend, twist and turn.

MY HEAD

My head is a very important part of me because it holds
my brain. I think, feel and remember with my brain.
My eyes, ears, mouth, nose and skin tell
my brain what is happening
in the world outside.

I smell and
breathe through
the two holes
in my nose.
These are
called nostrils.

My lips and tongue help
me to talk and to taste
different flavours.

My neck holds
up my head.
The muscles
in my neck are
very strong.

My brain is like a computer. It is my body's control centre. Messages are sent between my brain and all the different parts of my body.

My nose tells my brain what I am smelling.

This is my windpipe: it takes air to my lungs.

My tongue tastes my food and moves it around my mouth as I chew.

This is my foodpipe: it goes down to my tummy.

5

MY EYES

My eyes are like television cameras.
They send moving pictures of the world outside
back to my brain, which then works out what I can see.

My eyelashes help
to stop dust getting
into my eye.

This black circle is
my pupil. It is really
a window that lets
light into my eye.

My eyelids are like curtains.
They cover my eyes when
I sleep and when I blink.
I blink about 15 times a minute.

This is my eyeball.
Inside is a kind of clear jelly.
It keeps my eyeball round and smooth,
and light can pass through it.

Like a camera,
my eye has a lens
to help me to see
clearly and sharply.

Tears are made
in these special tubes.
Tears keep my eyes clean.
But nobody knows why we
cry tears when we are unhappy.

This nerve
carries the picture
from my eye back
to my brain.

MY EARS

All I can see are the outer ears on the sides of my head.
Most of my ear is out of sight inside my head.
This hidden part of my ear sends messages to my brain,
telling me what I can hear.

The outer part of my
ear is like a funnel.
It directs sounds into
my ear passage.

There are no bones in this
part of my ear. I can bend
it like a piece of rubber.

I have one ear on
either side of my head.
Two ears help me to tell
exactly where sounds
are coming from.

This is my eardrum.
When a sound hits this
piece of skin, it vibrates
just like a drum.

These three small
bones carry the vibration
through to my inner ear.

This is my inner ear.
The nerves in here tell my
brain what I am hearing.

MY CHEST

When I run very fast I can feel a thumping in my chest.
This is my heart beating. Sometimes I get really puffed and then
I breathe in all the air I can.

These are my nipples.
Mothers use them to feed
their babies with milk.
Children and men do
not use their nipples.

When I put my hand
here I can feel my
heart beating.

When I put my
hand here, I can
see and feel my
chest going up and
down as I breathe.

I breathe in air through my nose and mouth. The air comes down my windpipe and fills up my lungs.

This is my heart. It keeps my blood moving all around my body. My blood never stays still; it is always moving.

Here are my lungs. They take in oxygen from the air. I need oxygen to keep me alive.

This big flat muscle is my diaphragm. It holds up my lungs.

MY TUMMY

When I am hungry my tummy feels empty and I can hear it rumbling. When I have eaten a lot it feels stretched and full.

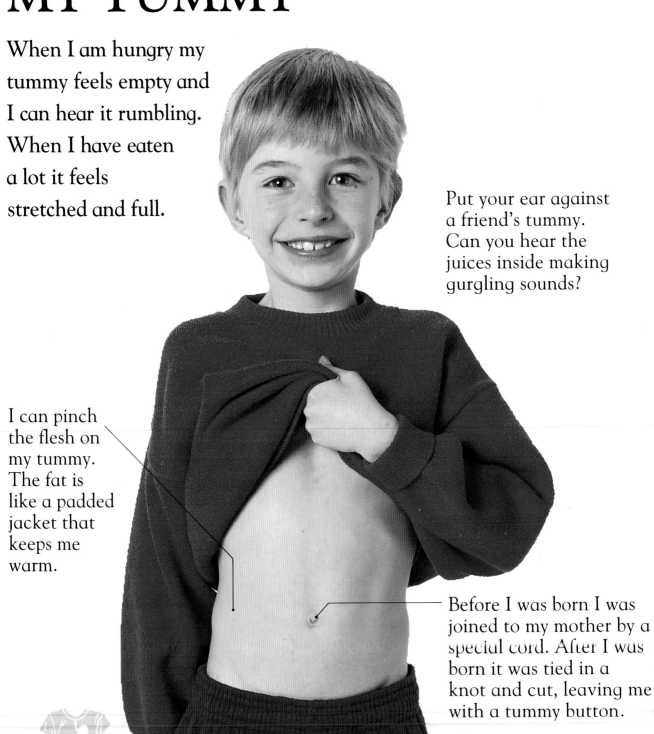

Put your ear against a friend's tummy. Can you hear the juices inside making gurgling sounds?

I can pinch the flesh on my tummy. The fat is like a padded jacket that keeps me warm.

Before I was born I was joined to my mother by a special cord. After I was born it was tied in a knot and cut, leaving me with a tummy button.

The food that I swallow goes on a long journey through my body. On the way, all the good things that my body needs are passed through to my blood.

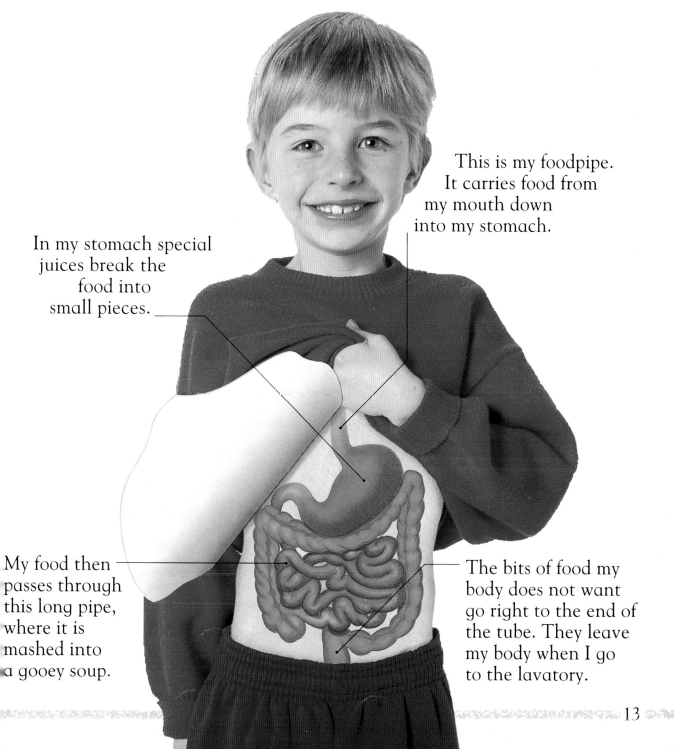

This is my foodpipe. It carries food from my mouth down into my stomach.

In my stomach special juices break the food into small pieces.

My food then passes through this long pipe, where it is mashed into a gooey soup.

The bits of food my body does not want go right to the end of the tube. They leave my body when I go to the lavatory.

MY LEGS AND ARMS

I use my legs and feet to walk, run and jump.

I use my arms to push, pull and carry.

My elbow is where my arm bends and straightens.

My knee is where my leg bends. Is your knee knobbly or smooth?

Exercise helps to keep my muscles supple and strong.

My ankle lets me wiggle and twist my foot from side to side.

My toes help me to balance and bend my foot as I walk.

Muscles help me move my bones.
I have muscles all over my body.
They are joined to my bones by long
stretchy bands called tendons.

I have muscles to
move my hand...

...muscles to bend and
straighten my arm...

When I bend my
arm, the muscle
bunches up. When
I stretch it, the
muscle flattens out.

...big thigh and calf
muscles to move my leg...

...and muscles to
move my foot.

MY HANDS

I can wave, draw and pick up all sorts of things with my hands.
I use my hands to feel things too. The skin on my fingertips
can feel even the tiniest grain of sand.

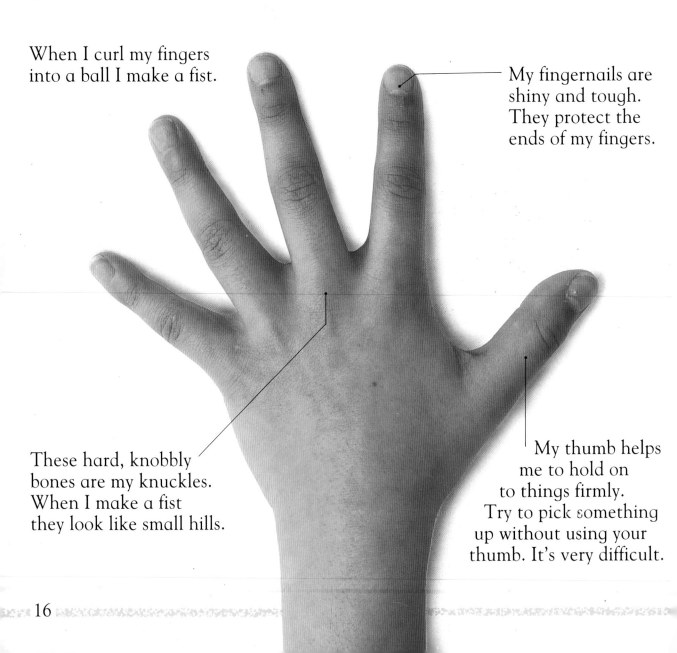

When I curl my fingers
into a ball I make a fist.

My fingernails are
shiny and tough.
They protect the
ends of my fingers.

These hard, knobbly
bones are my knuckles.
When I make a fist
they look like small hills.

My thumb helps
me to hold on
to things firmly.
Try to pick something
up without using your
thumb. It's very difficult.

16

The nerves in my fingertips
feel all sorts of things –
hot and cold, hard and soft,
rough and smooth.

My fingers are
worked by tendons,
which are like pieces
of string attached
to my fingerbones.

The many small
bones that make
up my wrist are
held together by
stretchy bands
called ligaments.

17